ECMAScript 6

Learn One of The Most Powerful

Scripting Languages that is

implemented in the Form of JavaScript,

JScript and ActionScript

Daniel Green

Disclaimer

While all attempts have been made to verify the information provided in this book, the author doesn't assume any responsibility for errors, omissions, or contrary interpretations of the subject matter contained within. **The information provided in this book is for educational and entertainment purposes only. The reader is responsible for his or her own actions and the author does not accept any responsibilities for any liabilities or damages, real or perceived, resulting from the use of this information.**

Contents

Book Description

This book explores ECMAScript 6(ES6) in detail. It begins by explaining what ES6, its origin, is and how it is used and where it is used. ES6 has issues when it comes to compatibility with browsers. This book will guide you on how to run ES6 on a browser which is incompatible.

The *"Let"* keyword, which was introduced for the first time in ES6 has been discussed in detail in this book, thus, you will understand how to use it. The keyword *"const"*, which is also a new feature in Javascript is also discussed. This book will guide you on how you can play around with variables using this keyword as well as what you should not do in order to avoid errors.

After reading this book, you will be able to use a single function to return multiple values in ES6. Arrow functions, which were introduced for the first time in ES6, are also discussed. This book will also guide you in how to create and instantiate classes in ES6.

The following topics have been explored in this book:

- Promise vs. Callback

- The "catch" function

- Creating modules

Introduction

The development of Javascript was solely based on ECMAScript (ES). This is a scripting language which is used on the client side of the web. The language introduced numerous features which programmers can use to develop complex libraries. ECMAScript comes in different versions.

During the release of ES4, many features were announced that they will be releasing in the future versions of the same language. These features were then implemented in ES6. They served as solution to the problems that programmers experienced while developing websites using ECMAScript version 5 (ES5).

Chapter 1: Definition

ECMAScript is a scripting language used on the client-side of the web. It is usually implemented in the form of Javascript, ActionScript or Jscript. The release of ECMAScript 6(ES6) was preceded by and replaced ES5. It reintroduced most of the features which were proposed in ES4. Javascript, which is a very popular programming language is solely based on ECMAScript. It comes in different editions, and these show some differences from one another. ECMAScript standard is very compatible with Javascript.

Javascript is used by programmers in the development of complex web applications. ES6 was developed so as to provide programmers with a language for creating libraries, complex libraries and code generators.

It is important for you as a programmer to know the features of ES6 which can be supported in the versions of browsers which are currently in use. ECMAScript 6 brought numerous changes on ES5 ranging in their scope from small to big. Among these changes, the language has a new syntax.

Chapter 2 How to Run ECMAScript 6 a Browser which is Incompatible

If you want to write ES6 for your site on a development phase, then you need to embed "Traceur" compiler on your browser. This will then have the task of compiling your ES6 code into Javascript which can be supported in simple browsers on the fly.

To embed Traceur in your website, use the following code:

```
        <!doctype html>
<html>
  <head>...</head>
  <body>
    ...
    <!—Loading the Traceur Compiler -->
    <script src="https://google.github.io/traceur-compiler/bin/traceur.js"></script>
    <!-- Bootstrap.js will find the script tags having the type module and then compile them using interfaces being  provided by the traceur.js -->
    <script src="https://google.github.io/traceur-compiler/src/bootstrap.js"></script>
    <script type="module">
      //Add your ES6 code here
    </script>
  </body>
</html>
```

However, if you are in a production environment, doing this for every page load can consume time and resource which can negatively affect the performance of the site. This explains why you should use the Traceur's node compiler so as to do the compilation once and for all and embed the Javascript already compiled into your web pages. The following sections will explain how to do this.

Traceur comes with a shell script called *"traceur"* which can be used for compilation of Javascript code with ES6.

How to compile the files

Ensure that you have installed "Node" in your machine. This should be followed by creating a Javascript code with some ES6 features in it. The following example illustrates this:

```
// saluter.js
class Saluting {
sayHello(name = 'Anonymous') {
console.log(`Hello ${name}!`);
}
}
var saluter = new Saluter();
saluter.sayHello();
```

Just run the above code and you will be prompted to enter your name. In my case, I provided the name *"Mike"* and the following will be the output:

```
Hello Mike
```

To run the above program, you need to use the compiler. This can be done by running the following command on the command prompt:

./traceur --out out/saluter.js --script saluter.js

After running the above command, an *"out/"* directory will be created and it will have all the ES6 features already compiled. Note that if you provide input files to the command line compiler, then they will be interpreted as anonymous modules. However, it is possible to treat them as global code (script). This can be done by using either one or several "--*script <filename>*" command line flags. If you need to test the previous *"saluter.js"* file, then use the following HTML page:

```
<html>
<head>
<script src="bin/traceur-runtime.js"></script>
<script src="out/saluter.js"></script>
</head>
<body>
You should see "Hi name!" on your console.
```

```
</body>
</html>
```

In the next sections, we are going to explore the new features which have been introduced in ES6.

Chapter 3 The "Let" Keyword

This keyword was introduced for the first time in ES6. With this keyword, one can create a bracket scope (block scope" variables in Javascript). Initially, only global variables and variable scope were supported in Javascript. However, this was advanced in ES6. Consider the following example:

```
       if(true)
{
   let y = 15;
   alert(y); //alert's 15
}
alert(y); //y is undefined here
```

Just write and run the above program. You will observe the following as the output:

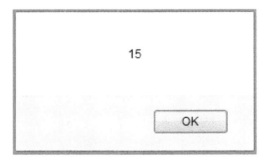

The above figure shows the first dialog of the output. Click on the "Ok" button and observe the resulting output. It will be an error and you will be told that "*y is undefined*". The reason is because of the scope.

With the "*let*" keyword, the accessibility of a variable is limited to a block, expression or statement. Use this keyword if you want to achieve this in your program.

Chapter 4 The *"const"* Keyword

This keyword was introduced for the first time in ES6 as well. With this keyword, it is possible for programmers to define variables which are read only in Javascript. By default, if you use this keyword while declaring your variable, then it becomes bracket scoped (or block scoped).

In any case, if you do a second declaration of a variable with the *"const"* keyword, then you will get an error. Consider the following example:

```
const y = 15;
//we have created the variable y in the above line and
we have used the //"const" keyword. The below line
will lead to an error because we are //declaring the
same variable a second time.
const y = 14;
if(true)
{
    //the constant ":y" is available in this scope but not
defined in it. The line //below will not cause an error
but a new "y" has been defined in this scope.
        const y = 14;

    //the below variable "x" will be accessible in this
scope but not outside
        const x = 12;
}
//here, we have created a new "here, we have created
a new "x" but no error will result because we do not
```

have another x defined in the scope(i.e., global
//scope)
const x = 12;

Just write the above program as it is and then try to run it.

For the case of the variable "*y*", the following error is
produced:

```
traceured.js:3:7: Duplicate declaration, y
```

The error shows that the variable has been declared more than

once in the same scope, which is not allowed after using the

"*const*" keyword. All what you need to know is that you cannot

re-declare a variable if you have declared it in the same scope.

Chapter 5 Function to Return Multiple Values

In Javascript, there are multiple ways you can use a single function to return multiple values. In ES6, it is easy to do this. Consider the program given below which shows how a function can return multiple values in ES6:

```
function fname()
{
   return [1, 2, 3, 4, 5, 7]; //we want to store our
variables in an array and then return the created
array.
}
var a, b, c, d, e, f;
//we are assigning the returned values to variables by
use of the ES6's array destructuring feature.
//let us ignore index 2 and 4 of our array.
[a, b, , d, , f] = fname();

alert(a);//a is at index 0
```

Just write the above program and then run it. You will observe the following as the output from the program:

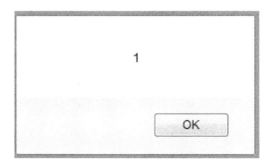

What we have done is that we have stored our values in an array. We have then assigned these values to the variables. On returning the value at index zero (0), we get 1 as the result. Note that arrays begin at index zero (0). Make sure that you understand how we have stored the values in the array and how we have assigned the values to variables. We have also used the variable so as to output our final result. Suppose we changed the program to the following:

```
function fname()
{
return [1, 2, 3, 4, 5, 7]; //we want to store our
variables in an array and then return the created
array.
}
var a, b, c, d, e, f;
//we are assigning the returned values to
variables by use of the ES6's array destructuring
feature.
//let us ignore index 2 and 4 of our array.
[a, b, , d, , f] = fname();
alert(f);//a is at index 5
```

What we are trying to do is to output the value which is stored in the 5th index of our array. The above program will then give us the following result:

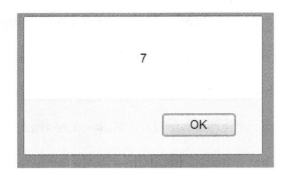

The figure shows that the value 7 is stored at the 5th index of our array. What you need to know is that ES^ can allow you to use variables to refer to the values stored in an array. It is also possible to ignore some of the values stored in the array as we have done in the example above.

Chapter 6 Default Function Arguments Values

Object destructuring, which is a new feature in ES6 allows us to create default values for the arguments of a function. It provides a syntax similar to the one for object destructuring which can be used to assign values to properties of objects. Consider the example given below:

```
var myobject = {a: 14, b: 50};
//matching the names of the properties of objects
with global variables for //assigninjg.
var {b, a, c} = myobject;
alert(a); //the value of a is 14
a = 35;
alert(a); //the value of a is 35
alert(myobject.a); //myobject.a is 14
alert(c); //c is undefined
```

Just write the above program and then run. Observe the output that you get which should be as follows:

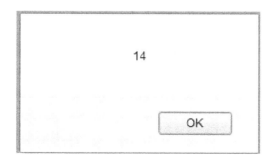

The above figure shows the first dialog which should appear after running the project. Note that we initialized the value of "*a*" to 14 and this explains the source of the output. Just click on the "*ok*" button and observe the next output. It will be as follows:

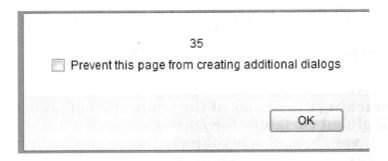

Notice how we assigned the value of "*a*" in our program to be 35. This explains the source of the output shown in the above figure. Again, click on the "*ok*" button and observe the next dialog which will appear. It should be as follows:

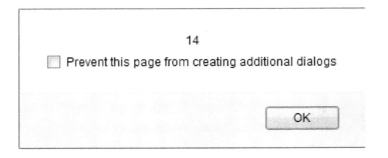

The above shows the result of "*myobject.a*". It is returning the initial value of the variable "*a*" rather than the second value. Again, click on the "*ok*" button and then observe the next dialog which will appear. It will be as follows:

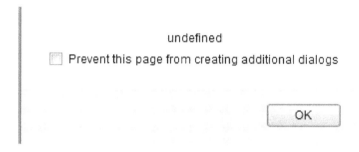

Clicking on the button again will result to no other dialog. Notice that we are trying to get the value of "*c*". However, we did not define its value and this explains the source of the last result shown in the figure. To create default function arguments using this feature the following should be done:

```
//An equal sign rather than the colon has been
used for the default object. The inside part of the
object will be as usual.
function fname({a = 14, b = 15} = {})
{
    alert(a); //the value of a is 14
    alert(b); //the value of b is 20
```

```
}
fname({b: 20});
```

Again, write the above program and then run it. You will observe the following output from the program:

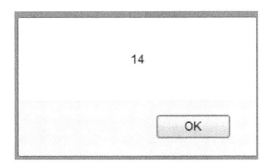

The above figure shows the result from the line "*alert(a)*". Notice that we initialized the value of this constant to 14. This explains the source of the above output. Click on the "*ok*" button and then observe the next dialog which will appear. It should be as follows:

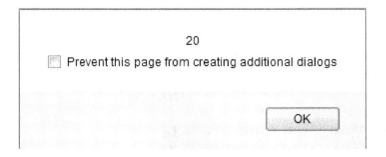

The above figure shows the result from the line "*alert(b)*".

Notice that it has given the last value of the variable rather the

initial value, which we declared at the beginning of the

program. This is how default function arguments can be

created in ES6.

Chapter 7 "..." Operator

This operator was first introduced in ES6 and it is called the spread operator. It is mostly used together with arrays to expand its variables syntax-wise. When this operator is used with an argument of a function, the function argument will then behave like an array of arguments.

If you need to have an indefinite number of arguments, then you can use this operator. The following sample program explains how the operator can be used:

```
//argmnts variable is just an array which holds
the passed function arguments
function fone(...argmnts)
{
    console.log(argmnts);
    console.log(argmnts.length);
}
fone(1, 3);
fone(1, 3, 6);
fone(1, 3, 6, 0);
function ftwo(x, y, ...argmnts)
{
    console.log(argmnts);
    console.log(argmnts.length);
}

//"argmnts" will hold only 6 and 8
function_two(1, 4, 6, 8);
```

Before this operator was introduced, programmers used "Array.prototype.slice.call" for the purpose of retrieving extra passed arguments. Consider the example program given below:

```
// argmnts variable is just an array which holds
the passed function
function fone()
{
  var argmnts =
Array.prototype.slice.call(arguments, fone.length);

  console.log(argmnts);
  console.log(argmnts.length);
}
fone(1, 3);
fone(1, 3, 6);
fone(1, 3, 6, 0);
function ftwo(x, y)
{
  var argmnts =
Array.prototype.slice.call(arguments, ftwo.length);
  console.log(argmnts);
  console.log(argmnts.length);
}
//"argmnts" holds only  6 and 8
ftwo(1, 4, 6, 8);
```

Applying the operator "..." to an array expands it into multiple variables terms of syntax. This is demonstrated in the code shown below:

```
        function fname(x, y)
{
   console.log(x+y);
}
var myarray = [1, 5];

fname(...myarray); //This is equal to fname(1, 5)
```

Chapter 8 *"class"* Keyword

This keyword was introduced in ES6 so that programmers can create classes in Javascript. In the earlier versions of Javascript, programmers used the constructor function. Once you have created your class, it is possible to define objects which are part of the same class. Consider the following program which demonstrates how this can be done:

```
    class Person
{
  //creating a constructor for the class
  constructor(name, sex)
  {
    //"this" is used to point to the current object
    this.name = name;
    this._sex = sex;
  }
  //defining a member function
  gName()
  {
    return this.name;
  }
  sName(name)
  {
    this.name = name;
  }
  //the above functions will make the function
accessible like a variable. They have been used as
wrappers around the other variables.
  setSex(value)
  {
```

```javascript
        this._age = value;
    }
    getSex()
    {
        return this._sex;
    }
}
//class student inherits person class
class Student extends Person
{
    constructor(name, age, class)
    {
        //this will point to the student class
        this.class = class;
        //calling the constructor of a super class. "super"
is used to point to a super class object
        super(name, sex);
    }
    getClass()
    {
        return this.class;
    }
    //overriding
    gName()
    {
        // calling the function gName function which is a
function in the supper //class
        return super.gName();
    }
}
//instance of person class
var pers = new Person("Mike", male);
//instance of student class
var st = new Student("Mike Artemov", 20, "Russia");
p.sex = male; //executes the setter
console.log(pers.sex); //executes the getter
```

You can write the program above and the run it. The output should be as follows:

```
Mike male
Mike Artemov 20 Russia
```

The figure shows that our program has run successfully. The first output is for the person named "Mike" who's sex is "male". The second output shows a student named "Mike Artemov", who's age is 20 and comes from Russia. Notice how we have defined our class using the "*class*" keyword. You should also note how we have instantiated our classes so as to create objects of the same type as the class.

Chapter 9 The Arrow "=>" Function

With ES6, there is a new way for programmers to create or define functions which are only a single statement. This is done by use of the arrow or lambda function. The arrow function is created as follows:

```
//addition is the name of the function
//a and b are the parameters of the function
var addition = (a, b) => a + b;
console.log(addition(3, 5)); //8
```

In the above function, the result should be the addition of the values of the two parameters. The value of "*a*" is 3 while that of "*b*" is 5. Adding these two should give you 8, which will form our output as shown below:

```
8
```

After executing arrow functions, the returned result is always the value of the statement. Although it is possible for you to write multiple statements in an arrow function, they are generally meant for writing of a single statement. Consider the following program example:

```
    var addition = (a, b) => {
a = a + 5;
b = b + 5;
return a + b;
}
    console.log(addition(5, 5)); //20
```

The program demonstrates how arrow function can be used to run multiple statements at a go. The program returns 20 as the result as you can see in the figure shown below:

20

Arrow functions can be used anywhere we use a regular Javascript function object since this is what they return. An example is a callback. Arrow functions can be used in this as shown below:

```
    function addition(x, y)
{
    console.log(x() + y()); //87
}
addition(p => 20 + 10, q => 1 + 56); // passing of two
function objects
```

This function will return 87 once executed.

Another feature of arrow function is the use of pointer "this". This pointer indicates the scope inside where it was passed as a callback if it is used inside a function which is executed asynchronously. For the case of regular functions, the pointer will point to the global scope when the execution is done asynchronously. This is demonstrated in the example given below:

```
    window.height = 20;
function Man(){
 this.height = 28;
 setTimeout(() => {
  console.log(this.height); //28
 }, 1100);
 setTimeout(function(){
  console.log(this.height); //20
 }, 1100);
}
var m = new Man();
```

Notice how we have used the pointer so as to access the values of the parameter *"height"* in our program.

Chapter 10 The "for of" Loop

This loop was introduced for the first time in ES6. It allows you as the programmer to iterate a collection of elements. Note that this loop will iterate over the values of the elements but not on the keys. Here, the collection can be either a set, a list, an array, or even a custom collection of objects. In the earlier versions of Javascript and before the introduction of ES6, programmers used either the *"for"* or the *"for each"* loop to iterate a collection of elements. Note that an iterator is a construct in programming which can allow you to visit each and every element contained in a collection.

Using "for of" to iterate through an array

The following program example demonstrates how to iterate an array using the "for of" loop:

```
     var myArray = [1, 2, 3, 4, 5];
//'j' references the values stored in the indexes of the
array
for(var j of myArray)
{
   console.log(j); //1, 2, 3, 4, 5
}
```

The above program will produce the elements of the array. You can write and run it and you will observe the following output:

```
1 2 3 4 5
```

The key "*symbol.iterator*" is necessary for a collection of objects to be iterated using the "*for of*" loop.

Using the "for of" loop to iterate a custom collection object

Our aim is to implement the property "*symbol.iterator*" on our collection of objects. The property always returns an object with the "*next()*" property, that is, the iterator object. Consider the following code sample which demonstrates this:

```
    var ccollection = {
elements: [1, 2, 3, 4,5],
size : 4 ,
pointer :0,
[Symbol.iterator]:  function(){
  var elm = this.elements;
  var sz = this.size;
  var pn = this.pointer;
  return{
    next: function() {
      if(pn > sz)
      {
         return { value: undefined, done: true };
      }
```

```
        else
        {
           pn++;
           return { value: elm[pn - 1], done: false };
        }
      },
   };
  }
}
for(var j of ccollection)
{
   console.log(j); //1, 2, 3, 4, 5
}
```

Just write the above code and then run it. You will observe the
following output:

```
1 2 3 4 5
```

Chapter 11 The "yield" Keyword and "function*()" Syntax

ES6 introduced a new feature called the Javascript Generators. This is made up of both the *"yield"* keyword and *"function()*"*. Generators are responsible for providing a way in which Javascript functions can return a collection. It also provides a way for the elements of the returned collection to be iterated. Previously, Javascript generators were used as follows:

```
        function cname()
{
   return [1, 2, 3, 4,5];
}
var collection = cname();
for(var j = 0; j < collection.length; j++)
{
   console.log(collection[j]);
}
```

You can write and then run the above program. The output will just be the previous ones in which the elements of the array are outputted. This is shown below:

```
1 2 3 4 5
```

With Generators, however, this can be done as follows:

```
    function* cname()
{
  yield 1;
  yield 2;
  yield 3;
  yield 4;
    yield 5;
}

for(var j  of cname())
{
  console.log(j);
}
```

Just write the program and then run it. The following output will be observed:

```
1 2 3 4 5
```

What happens is that Javascript creates an object having "*symbol.iterator*" property from the values which have been yielded. The "*for of*" construct then uses these values for iteration purpose.

Chapter 12 "0o" Literal

This is a new way for programmers to create octal values in Javascript. It was first introduced in ES6. During the earlier versions of Javascript and before the release of ES6, programmers were forced to place a zero (0) in front of numbers to indicate that they are octal values. Javascript stores octal and hexadecimal numbers as binary after converting them into decimal. Consider the sample program given below:

```
//Before the release of ES6
var x = 012;
console.log(x);
//ES6
var y = 0o12;
console.log(y);
```

Notice the difference in the two ways above, before ES6 and after ES6. The following output will be observed from the program:

```
10
10
```

This shows that ES6 has made it easy for one to identify octal numbers.

Chapter 13 The "ob" Literal

With this literal, it is possible to directly create a binary of a number by use of its literal. In the earlier versions of Javascript, programmers provided the number in a decimal format which was then converted into a binary format before being stored in the memory. This has changed since ES6 was developed, the number can be directly specified in a binary format. Consider the example given below:

var x = 0b11011101;
console.log(x);

Just write the above as it is written above and the run it. You will observe the following output:

```
221
```

As shown in the figure, the conversion was successful and it has been done very easily.

Chapter 14 The "Set" Object

This is just a collection of keys which are unique. In Javascript a key is a primitive sort of object reference data type. With arrays, it is possible for you to store duplicate keys. However, this is not possible with sets. This marks their difference. The following program demonstrates how you can work with set object including adding keys, deleting keys and finding their size:

```
    //creating a set
var mySet = new Set();
//adding a total of three rows to the set
mySet.add({x: 12});
mySet.add(44);
mySet.add("sample");
//checking whether the key being provided is present
console.log(mySet.has("sample"));
//deleting a key
mySet.delete(44);
//iterate or loop the keys in the set
for(var j of mySet)
{
    console.log(j);
}
//create a set from array values
var mySet_1 = new Set([1, 2, 3, 4, 5]);
//getting size of the set
console.log(mySet_1.size); //5
//creating a clone of just another set
var mySet_2 = new Set(mySet.values());
```

Notice the procedure and what we have done in the above example. We have created our set and then we have added three keys to it. We have then checked whether the set has the key "*sample*". The result will be a positive one since we added this key to our set. We have also deleted the key "*44*" from our set which is one of the keys we had inserted into it. That is how we use the "*set*" object in ES6.

Chapter 15 Set vs. WeakSet in ES6

These two are used in Javascript for the purpose of
storing a collection of keys which are unique. However, the
two are not the same; there are some differences in how they
work and how they can be used. The following are some of
these differences:

1. They show different behavior whenever an object
    referenced by their keys gets deleted. Consider the
    program shown below:

    ```
    var mySet = new Set();
    var weakSet = new WeakSet();
    (function(){
      var x = {p: 14};
      var y = {q: 14};
      mySet.add(x);
      weakSet.add(y);
    })()
    ```

    Pointer "*y*" will be deleted by the garbage collector.

    This means that "*q:14*" will be removed from the

    memory. However, the pointer "*x*" will not be

    deleted nor will "*p:14*" be removed from the

memory. This is because we have used a *"set"* rather than *"weakSet"*. With *"set"*, we can have more garbage in memory compared to *"weakSet"*. The reason is because the references for *"set"* are stronger pointers compared to the ones for *"weakSet"* which are weak pointers.

2. Note that the keys for *"weakSet"* cannot be of primitive type. *Consider the example given below:*

```
var mySet = new Set([1,2,3,4]);
//wekset cannot be created from another set or an array
var weakset = new WeakSet();
weakset.add({x: 1}); //referencing to an object
```

The above program shows that it is impossible to create a "weakSet" from either an array or another set.

3. With "weakSet"s, there are no functions or methods which can be applied on a whole set of keys. An example of this is looping and size. Consider the sample program given below:

```
var mySet = new Set([1,2,3,4,5]);
//impossible to create weakest from an array.
```

```
var weakset = new WeakSet();
weakset.add({x: 1}); //referencing to an object
console.log(mySet.size);//5
console.log(weakset.size);//undefined
for(var j of mySet)
{
    console.log(j); //1,2.3.4.5
}
//throws error will not be executed
for(var j of weakset)
{
    console.log(j);
}

mySet.clear();
weakset.clear(); //This will work
```

Just write the program as it is here and then run it. You will observe the following as the output from the program:

```
5
undefined
1,2.3.4.5
```

The first line of the output shows the result of the command "mySet.size". This is the size of the set which is has 5 elements. This explains the source of the first line of the output. The second line of the output shows the result from the line "*weakest.size*". Note that the weakest has got no keys in it, so we cannot get its size. This explains the source of the second line of the output. The third line of the output gives the elements stored in the set "*mySet*". We iterated through these elements or keys using the variable "*j*". Note how this has been done. You are now aware of some of the differences between the two.

Chapter 16 The "Map" Object

This is made up of a collection of keys which are unique together with their values. The keys and the values can be of primitive types or just object references. In 2D arrays, programmers are able to store duplicate values. However, doing this in a map will result into an error. This explains the difference between the two.

With "set" in Javascript, one can store only the keys but in the "map", one can store both the keys and the value pairs. The program given below shows how to create a "map" object, add keys, find size, delete keys and other functionalities:

```
//creating a map
var myMap = new Map();
//create three keys and their values and then add
them to the map
myMap.set({a: 14}, 14);
//Let us overwrite the same key
myMap.set(43, 14);
myMap.set(43, 13);
//check whether the key being provided is available
console.log(myMap.has(43)); //This is true
//retrieving the key
console.log(myMap.get(43)); //14
//deleting a key
myMap.delete(43);
//iterate or loop through the keys contained in the
```

```
map.
for(var j of myMap)
{
    console.log(j);
}
//deleting all the keys
myMap.clear();
//creating a map from the arrays.
var myMap_1 = new Map([[1, 2], [4, 5]]);
//size of the map
console.log(myMap_1.size); //This will return 2
```

Notice that we have begun by adding three keys to our map.

These keys also have values associated with them. We have

also overwritten keys which are the same. Notice we have

inserted the key 43 into the map. We then check whether this

key is present or not. The result will be positive since we

already have it. We then deleted this key from our map.

Next was the creation of variable "j" which we have used

to loop through the contents of our map. Our aim is to retrieve

the keys already in our map. This will then give us the

following output:

a 13

14 is not part of the output because we deleted it and its

key from our map. The last thing which we have done is to

delete all of the keys contained in the map. You now know how to create and add keys and their values into a map, how to check whether a certain key is present in a map, and also how to delete keys from a map. Our map now contains no key since we have deleted all those that were available.

Chapter 17 "Map" vs. "WeakMap"

These two were both introduced in ES6. Programmers use them to store unique keys together with their associated values. However, the two exhibit some differences which are discussed below:

1. They behave differently when an object referenced by their keys gets deleted. Consider the program shown below:

```
var myMap = new Map();
var weakmap = new WeakMap();
(function(){
  var x = {p: 12};
  var y = {q: 12};
  map.set(x, 1);
  weakmap.set(y, 2);
})()
```

{p:12} and {q:12} cannot be referenced anymore as shown in the program. What will happen is that the garbage collector will delete the key "y" pointer and removes {q:12} from the memory. Note that this is for weakMap. However, for the case of the map, the case will be different. The garbage collector will not delete "*x*" nor will {p:12} be removed from memory. This shows that with maps, more garbage can build up in the memory compared to weakMaps. The reason is because the references for maps are strong pointers while those for weakMaps are weak pointers.

2. The keys for a weakMap cannot be of primitive type, nor can they be by a 2D array. Consider the sample program given below:

```
myMap.set(43, 12);
//an invalid type error will be thrown
weakmap.set(43, 13);
//this will not work. Errors will be thrown
var myMap_1 = new WeakMap([[1, 4], [4, 6]]);
```

3. With weakMaps, there are no functions or methods which can be applied on a whole set of keys. An example of this is looping and size. Consider the sample program given below:

```
console.log(weakmap.size); //This is not defined
//create a loop for the map
for(var j of myMap)
{
   console.log(j);
```

```
}
//create a loop for the weakMap keys. This will
not work
for(var j of weakmap)
{
    console.log(j);
}
//deleting all the keys
myMap.clear();
weakmap.clear(); //this will work
```

All you need to know is that you cannot loop

through the elements of a weakMap unlike in a map.

Chapter 18 The "then" Function

This function belongs to the Javascript *"promise()"* object. With this object programmers are able to asynchronously call or execute a function. It was first introduced in ES6. In Javascript, there are many ways you can create a function asynchronously. However, there are no predefined ways of doing it. Most programmers use *"setTimeOut()"* for this purpose. The following function demonstrates how this can be done:

```
    function f1()
{
   console.log("Function called asynchronously");
}
setTimeout(f1, 0);
```

Just write the above program and then run it. You will observe the following output from the program:

function called asynchronously

OK

In ES6, this can be done as follows using both the "*promise()*" object and the "*then()*" function:

```
        function f1(rslve, reject)
{
  console.log("Function called");
   rslve();
}
//function f1 will be referenced by "then" property
and then executed asynchronously.
var promise = new Promise(f1);
function status()
{
   console.log("It was sucessful");
}
 function error(er)
{
   console.log(er);
}
promise.then(status, error);
```

The object and the function must be used together as the function provides the implementation. The execution of the function "*then()*" is done asynchronously meaning that it will apply to the callbacks. What we have done is to passd two callbacks to the function "*then()*". These are the "*rslve*" and "*reject*" callbacks.

If the asynchronous operation runs successfully, then the "*rslve*" callback will be called. If it runs unsuccessfully, then the *"reject"* callback will be called. In this case, an error object will also be called. Consider the following example programs which explain further on how to use these:

```
    var promiseObject = new
Promise(function(rslv, reject){
   rslv(2);
   //this will beignored
   return 6;
});
function errr(er)
{
   console.log(er);
}
function status(value)
{
   console.log(value);
   return 1;
}
promiseObject.then(status, errr).then(status, errr);
```

Just write and run the above program. The following output will be observed:

```
2
1
```

Below is another program which demonstrate how object *"promise()"* and function *"then()"* can be used:

```
    var promiseObject = new
Promise(function(rslv, reject){
   reject("An error occurred");
});
```

```
function errr(er)
{
    console.log(er);
}
function status()
{
    console.log("It was successful");
}
promiseObject.then(status, errr).then(status, errr);
```

Just write the program as it is above and then run it. The following will be observed as the output:

```
An error occurred
It was successful
```

Chapter 19 Promise vs. Callback

A callback is a function which is passed to another function. Programmers can choose to execute or call functions synchronously or asynchronously. Consider the example program given below:

```
function f()
{
   return 2;
}
function a(b)
{
   //execute b
   return b();
}
alert(a(f));
```

Write the program just as it is above and then run it. You will observe the following output:

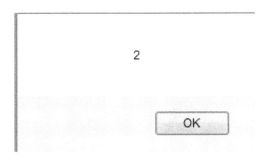

What we have done is create a function "*f*". This function has then been passed as a callback to the function "*a*". The function "a" has the option of executing it either synchronously or asynchronously. In this case, the callback has been executed asynchronously.

A promise object works by taking a callback and then executing it asynchronously. This is demonstrated below:

```
        function f()
{
   return 2;
}
 function errr(er)
{
   alert(er);
}
var promiseObject = new Promise(function(cback,
er){
   alert(cback());
});
promiseObject.then(f, errr);
```

We have created a function "*f*". This has then been used with the promise function "*then()*" . This function was then executed asynchronously. You will observe the following output from the program:

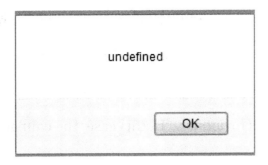

Chapter 20 The "catch" Function

With the *"promise()"* object in Javascript, programmers can wrap asynchronous operations and their associated events. Whenever a code is run asynchronous, there is a high chance that explicit or implicit exceptions will occur. In most programming languages, including Javascript, exceptions can be handled using the *"try...catch"* block. However, the promise object comes with a more easy and convenient way of doing this. The following example illustrates how we can handle an exception inside the *"then()"* function:

```
var promiseObject = new
Promise(function(rslv, reject){
  try
  {
    throw "An Exception Occurred";
    rslv();
  }
  catch(exc)
  {
    alert(exc);
  }
});
function status()
{
  alert("The program ran successfully");
}
 function errr(er)
```

```
{
    alert(er);
}
promiseObject.then(status, errr);
```

Just write the program as it is and then run it. It will give you
the following as the output:

An Exception Occurred

OK

This is how it is done. However, with the promise object, it can
be done as follows:

```
        var promiseObject = new
Promise(function(rslv, reject){
    throw "An Exception occurred";
    rslv();
});
function status()
{
    alert("The program ran Successfully");
}
 function errr(er)
{
    alert(er);
}
```

```
function ctchd(ec)
{
   alert(ec);
}
promiseObject.then(status, errr).catch(ctchd);
```

Just write the above program and then run it. You will observe the following output:

An Exception Occurred

[OK]

This shows how we have achieved the same result but in different ways. It also explains how interesting it is to use ES6 for development due to its amazing features.

In case an exception occurs and you had not implemented the *"try...catch"* block in your program, the function *"then()"* handles the exception using the *"reject"* callback. The function *"then()"* also creates a promise object internally which will fire its own callback. A custom promise object is returned by the *"reject"*, then the function *"then()"*

will return that promise. If a *"reject"* is not found, then the promise will be stopped. Consider the following sample program:

```
var promiseObject = new
Promise(function(rslv, reject){
    throw "An Exception occurred";
    rslv();
});
function status()
{
    console.log("Function ran successfully");
}
function errr(er)
{
    alert(er);
}

promiseObject.then(status, errr).then(status, errr);
```

Again, write the above program just as it is and run it. The following output will be observed:

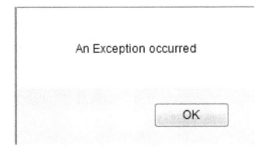

We have achieved the same result with the above program. This shows how dynamic ES6 is.

The "catch()" will always return a promise object as the result. It is also possible for the programmer to return a custom promise inside the catch, or it will create a new internal promise. The function *"then()"* will then fire the callback *"rslv"*. If anything else other than a promise object is returned inside the catch, then this will be ignored and the catch will create and return a promise instead. This is demonstrated in the program given below:

```
    var promiseObject = new
Promise(function(rslv, reject){
   throw "An Exception occurred";
   rslv();
});
function status()
{
   alert("The function ran Successfully");
}
 function errr(er)
{
alert(er);
}
function catched(ec)
{
   alert(ec);
}
promiseObject.then(status,
errr).catch(catched).then(status, errr);
```

Just write the above program the way it is written here and then run it. You will observe the following output:

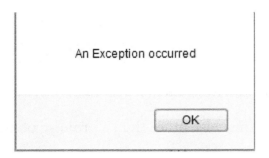

This is just the first dialog of the output. Click on the "*ok*" button. The following dialog will result:

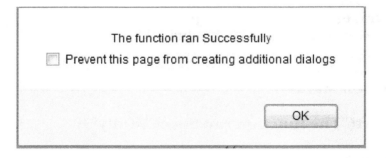

Chapter 21 Creating Modules

In Javascript, a module is just a collection of functions, objects or variables that provide the same or similar functionality. They can be used by other JS programs or modules. They help programmers to prevent global variables and to hide the details of how they have been implemented. They provide a way in which related Javascript codes can be grouped or packaged together.

It is possible that a library or file in Javascript could be a module. This happens if it prevents the overriding of global variables and hides how the functionality has been implemented. Let us discuss some of the different ways on how we can create modules:

1. Using the Immediately Invoke function expression- this function is anonymous and it invokes itself. This method was used in the early days of Javascript for creation of modules. Consider the following program which shows how this can be done:

```javascript
(function(window){
var add = function(p, q){
  return p + q;
}
var subtract = function(p, q){
  return p - q;
}
var maths = {
  findAddition: function(x, y){
    return sum(x,y);
  },
  findDifference: function(x, y){
    return sub(x, y);
  }
}
window.maths = maths;
})(window);
//Module ends here
alert(math.findAddition(1, 2));
alert(math.findDifference(1, 2));
```

Just write the program as it is above and then run it.

The observed output should be as follows:

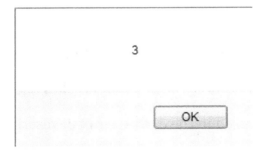

The above figure shows the result of the addition

operator. It adds 2 and 1 to get 3. Just click on the

"*ok*" button and observe what happens. The next dialog will be as follows:

```
                        -1
  ☐  Prevent this page from creating additional dialogs


                                    ┌──────────┐
                                    │    OK    │
                                    └──────────┘
```

The above result shows the difference after subtracting 2 from 1. The functions "*sum*" and "*sub*" have been kept in memory. However, we have prevented the occurrence of the overriding of global variables. However, the "*maths*" object is accessible from anywhere in the program. It hides how the functionality of the module has been implemented.

2. Using CommonJS- this is a Javascript specification which is not supported by any browser. NodeJS makes use of this in most cases. Let us create a file named "*file1.js*". We will also create another file and name it "*file2.js*". We will then use the file "*file1.js*"

as a module in the file *"file2.js"*. The following is the

code for the file *"file1.js"*:

```
var sum = function(p, q){
    return p + q;
}
var sub = function(p, q){
    return p - q;
}
var math = {
  findAddition: function(x, y){
    return sum(x,y);
  },
  findDifference: function(x, y){
    return sub(x, y);
  }
}
//Variables which intend to be used outside
should be members of "exports" object.
exports.math = math;
```

The following should be the code for *"file2.js"*:

```
//we do not require a file extension
    var math = require("./math").math;
    alert(math.findAddition(1, 2));
    Alert(math.findDifference(1, 2));
```

Notice that we have created the two files separately.

We then implemented the first file as a module in

the second file. We have tried as much as possible to

avoid overriding of global variables. We have also

hidden the implementation details as much as possible.

The program will give the following output once you run it:

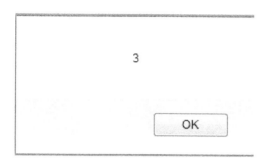

The above figure shows the result after adding 2 and 1. You need to know how the functions have been passed. Just click on the *"ok"* button and observe the next dialog. It should be as follows:

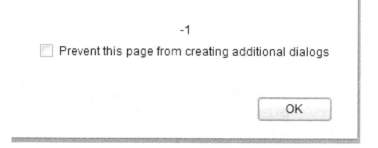

The above figure shows the result of subtracting 2 from 1 which is -1. It is possible to implement browser support in CommonJS but the performance issues will be numerous.

3. Defining modules asynchronously- AMD is a browser specification in Javascript and it is used for creation of modules. The designers of AMD take care of issues associated with the browser while developing it. Browsers will not entirely support AMD.

We want to create a program to demonstrate how RequireJS can be used for creation and importation of modules in Javascript. The following is the code:

```html
<!doctype html>
<html>
  <head></head>
  <body>
    <!—Load the library RequireJS and then provide the path where the JS files for your website are located. We do not require a file extension. -->
    <script type="text/javascript" src="http://requirejs.org/docs/release/2.1.16/minified/require.js" data-main="index"></script>
  </body>
</html>
```

After writing the above code, save it with the name "*file1.js*". We need to implement it in our second file as a module. The code should be as follows:

```
//the list of modules which are required
require(["math"], function(math){
    //the main program
    alert(math.findAddition(1, 2));
    alert(math.findDifference(1, 2));
})
```

Our final code should be as follows:

```
define(function(){
    var sum = function(p, q){
        return p + q;
    }
    var sub = function(p, q){
        return p - q;
    }
    var math = {
        findAddition: function(p, q){
            return sum(p, q);
        },
        findDifference: function(p, q){
            return sub(p, q);
        }
    }
    return math;
});
```

This how modules are created. In the main program we have greatly prevented global variables from being overridden and we have hidden how the functionality of the module has been implemented.

4. Universal module definition- UMD is one of the ways in which modules can be implemented and be importable using AMD, CommonJS and IIFE. Many techniques exist under UMD but you have the choice of using the one of your choosing. In this example, we will use returnExports pattern in order to demonstrate the use of this. Here is the code:

```
// the previous module can be simplified to the
    following if there exists no dependencies
    (function (root, factory) {
        //Detecting the environment
        if (typeof define === 'function' &&
    define.amd) {
            //the AMD
            define([], factory);
        } else if (typeof exports === 'object') {
            //the CommonJS
            module.exports = factory();
        } else {
            // Importing the script tag i.e., IIFE
            root.returnExports = factory();
        }
    }(this, function () {
        // Defining the module
        var sum = function(p, q){
            return p + q;
        }
        var sub = function(p, q){
```

```
    return p - q;
  }
  var math = {
    findAddition: function(p, q){
      return sum(p,q);
    },
    findDifference: function(p, q){
      return sub(p, q);
    }
  }
  return math;
}));
```

With UMD, you can create modules but not import them.

ES6 introduced ways for the modules to be supported within browsers. This was a step toward solving the problems involved in the creation of modules in the earlier versions of Javascript. The modules for ES6 can be supported everywhere. A file is used to represent modules in ES6. Consider the following example:

```
export class Math {
  constructor()
  {
    this.sum = function(p, q){
      return p + q;
    }
    this.sub = function(p, q){
```

```
            return p - q;
        }
    }
    findAddition(x, y)
    {
        return this.sum(x, y);
    }
    findSub(x, y)
    {
        return this.sub(x, y);
    }
}
```

To import the above module into the main program, do the following:

```
import {Math} from 'math';
    var math = new Math();
        alert(math.findSum(1, 2));
    alert(math.findSub(1, 2));
```

Write the program just the way it is here and then run it. You will observe the following as the output:

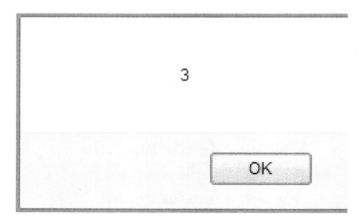

The above figure shows the result of adding 2 and 1.
Click on the "*ok*" button and then observe the next
dialog. It will be as follows:

-1

☐ Prevent this page from creating additional dialogs

| OK |

The above figure shows the result of subtracting 2
from 1. No other dialog will appear after clicking on
the "*ok*" button.

Conclusion

It can be concluded that ECMAScript 6 (ES6) brought so many changes to the Javascript programming language. The library was developed to solve the problems experienced by developers who used the earlier versions of Javascript. ES6 is mostly used for scripting on the client side of most websites. Its release was preceded by ES6 which showed many weaknesses. ES6 was intended to solve these weaknesses.

Most of the features implemented in this language were proposed earlier during the release of ES4. You need to note that Javascript is solely based on ECMAScript. As a developer, it is important for you to understand the various features of ES6 which are supported in browsers which are currently in use.

If you are developing your website and you want to run your code on your browser, then Traceur compiler needs to be embedded on your browser. However, this needs to be done for each of the web pages that you create.

This explains why you should use the Traceur node compiler. With this, you will have to embed it only one time.

What happens is that the compiler converts the ES6 code into Javascript code which is very compatible with the browsers.

ES6 introduced many new keywords into the field of programming. If you use the keyword "*const*" in declaration of your variable, then trying to create another variable with the same name in the same program will result into an error. It is also possible for programmers to create classes in ES6 using the "*class*" keyword. They will also be allowed to create instances of these classes. Arrow or lambda functions were also introduced in ES6 and with these, programmers are able to create functions which are only a single statement long.

www.ingramcontent.com/pod-product-compliance
Lightning Source LLC
Chambersburg PA
CBHW071010050326
40689CB00014B/3567